Train of Thought 2:
Almost Home

Also by Jason Wright

A Letter to the World (2015)

Train of Thought: Poems from the Red Line (2019)

Advanced Praise for *Train of Thought 2: Almost Home, More Poems from the Red Line*

"Jason Wright is a voice of richness, power, brilliance. He leads us into the dark of despair, wistfulness and longing only to offer up moments of hope, beauty and belonging. With every word Jason is a teacher—of life, of loss, and love.

Thank you for your authenticity. An honor to be let into your world so that I can better understand my own."

—Elaine Hall, Author of *Now I See the Moon: A Mother, A Son, and the Miracle of Autism*

"Jason's raw, vulnerable, and honest expression describing the depths of his despair will move you to the core and give you a strong appreciation for how writing can get you through even the darkest of times."

—Oryx Cohen, Producer of *Healing Voices*

"Like a spiritual push-pull mechanism, *Train of Thought 2* takes you almost home to that comfortable place of peace, away from 'medicated angels,' but then draws you back with Wright's unconquerable humor draped in his own neurodiversity and life rides tracked on the page. Wright leaves you on the edge of your seat, with a new-age, Kerouac-Simic free verse, but truly takes you home by not letting you arrive completely."

—Joshua Corwin, Author of *Becoming Vulnerable*

"This collection is not for the faint of heart. The poet bleeds like an open wound, you try to turn away, but you can't. Wright is courageous writer -- his poetry has a raw, sharp edge-and a straight-no-chaser sensibility."

—Doug Holder, Founder of *Ibbetson Street Pres*, Lecturer in Creative Writing, Endicott College

Train of Thought 2: Almost Home
More Poems from the Red Line

Jason Wright

another

publication

ISBN: 978-1-7339998-4-7
cover design TJ Edson
copyright 2021 creative commons

Library of Congress Control Number: 2021934293
First Edition, April, 2021

A little bit of history

These poems were written on the Red Line of the MBTA in Boston Massachusetts between the years 2010–2012. This is Part 2 of *Train of Thought, Poems from the Red Line*, if you remember the last stop was Charles M.G.H. This book picks up at Kendall, and we are halfway home. Prepare yourself, it's a full train of thought, and Davis Square is very far from where you are now.

Next stop Kendall.

For Lisa, and the City of Boston

STOPS TO HOME

PORTER

DAVIS (home)

Thank You

About the Author

Other *oddball* Publications

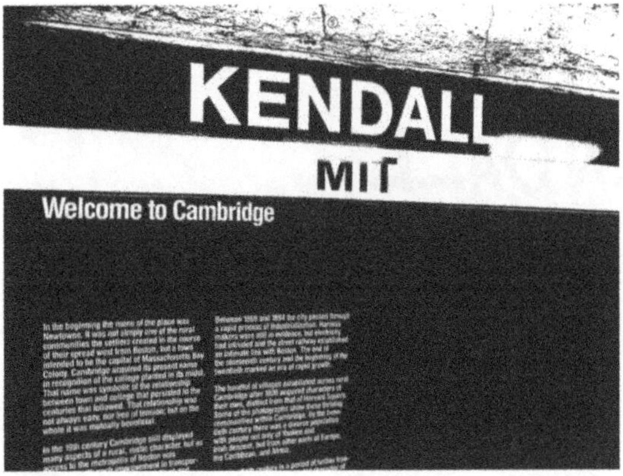
KENDALL
MIT
Welcome to Cambridge

KENDALL

RE: Born

I am re-born, my life maybe torn, I may have grown old.
The warmth has gone cold, but I am re: born.
Generated like a science age—
old,
but never told—
the science of self.
I learned today how much it takes for me to break down.

Learned today how to rebuild, in this world I live,
this mental dome, guarded by medicated angels,
each weathered word
passed down from me to her,
and she gets the finalized product, a project that
makes nothing seem like everything's gone wrong.
But the truth is
I'm learning to live.

It was raining, pouring down the remains of the day
onto my borrowed umbrella, "I'll promise I'll give it back
Marie."
I said, and got up from my desk to leave.
I wrote on a notepad:

Today is a new day.

When I see it tomorrow,
it will make me smile.

It will put me in the right place.

I just need to learn how to slow to a crawl.

Then Grouch and Eligh rock the track and I'm back
to writing the truth

I will let you know at the end of this book.

At the End of This Book

This book I live in has 365 pages.
So far, I'm on chapter 31.
I don't remember the last 25, It feels
like I'm only been awake and alive since 26.
Now, I am on my mission to change
what's written, to make the hero a villain
and the heroine
kill him.

Can you manage
the tragedies of life?

Boys are born and
grow old to watch their mother
and father die.
Then by that time
the little boy has grown
into a man and has his own fam,
so where am I
in this chapter?

I'm a freak of nature.
What's saved in a life overwhelmed with hatred?
The heat I feel all year long, until
my blood runs cold,
dripping off into the sidewalk—
dead blood don't clot,
it just washes away with the rain,
and all that's left is a strange stain
built and instrumented from someone's pain

or your own, as you scream at the walls.
You're not alone. I am.

You are...the man with the fam
and I'm stuck on this train—
a man made of sand.
Screaming at walls, wanting to write poems,
a letter to the world, but I am bleeding ink on
the sidewalk.

Dead men can't write,
it's almost time to stop.

Almost Time to Stop

In a moment's notice
Jekyll turns to Hyde.
Jekyll tries to hide.
In a minute St. Francis,
we will have a sangue witch
What am I writing?
This is madness.

(This is Madness)

Well, here I go again,
with a flow stupid and Zen—
like a box of matches.

We light, and unite,
the same stage,
with new players to play this game.

Some more people enter the train.
While I enter the Wu-tang.
Where I realize I have failed.

They have no idea, but see a
loose-leaf writer pounding
the pavement.
Wishing I could fly like a bird, or
a Frisbee, a boomerang I'll leave,
then my mind will travel free
and eventually come back to me.

It is this inertia, that stops you
and moves me.

I am just a diamond writing in London,
swimming like locusts, and sea shells
being risen to the top
to realize, no one cares about seashells.

And my mind retraces its steps to find
an answer, to a question I don't even know,
in a book called dramatist in dramedy.

This is
as good
as it gets folks,
choke on the melody
Let the tears fall freely.
We all have to be free. Dumb.
Free dumb, in this kingdom.
I am king dumb.
And off you go and
just like that I'll never see you again!

Friday is for Lovers

The weekend is for those in love.
They are reborn like winged angels
on a platform.
On a stage we act out this drama
The apartment floor is our curtain call.
The broken silence is our audience.
Our laughter is the curtains.
Our sadness conducts the show.
We are both alone.
We are both
                alone.
In our broken home.
You said to me that you have lowered
your expectations, congratulations.

But that's not a celebration.
That is your sadness and anger
about your current situation.
We have lived this length
for too long, our clothes
no longer fit us, our love
grows dust, our life stagnant.

Rust-colored-warmer-weather,
I wish we could start over,
but time does not rewind.
We are both older now.
And everyone has grown their love
into homes and happiness

And I just relent through
Heartbreak Poems
that have no home.

I will never read this to you
But I must rewrite my ending.
Because kisses on your crying eyes
make me write this.
Like were both stuck and refuse
to admit it.
That life is not a fairy tale princess.
A frog is still a frog
And a beast, a beast.
And at least my empty heart
will explode from the medications—
the lacerations from all that cigarette smoke.
And you can find yourself
Another lover, in a perfect world,
A world that is not pastels and paint brushes
I hope you'll find love, because I am too lost
to look.

Talking to the Man
Who Made Me

It was good to talk to you,
like lions,
roaring at each other
seeking dominance.
While letting the soft mane
and calm eyes prove
shadows in the
night.
We are stolen from the war.
We are broke and then sold.
We are forever alone.
But we are forever gold.
How much is gold worth
to them?

Free Prose

Sometimes we have to slow down
and see the scenery for what it is.
Fleeting.
Unless shot in to an image
or recorded like
a visual solo.
A strumming song
ends with the last string.
But pictures burn,
strings break.
And hearts break
and bend.
Lungs give out.
Knees go.
Neckties start to strangle
us whole,
like snakes
and guns.
Nooses.
Bracelets.
We wear to the end
and we remember
the noose.
You hung yourself with
the bracelet I wear for you.
The memory of figurines
dancing
behind an easel.
After all,
all this is—
is a puppet show.

Wrong Place

Listen to my words, friends.
Listen to the pen, scratching.
Listen to tapping, tap, tapping
on your chamber door.
It is only war, and nothing more.
My mind flies like birds.
Out of a volcano after a disrupting
eruption, a Pompeiic
aftermath
of flies,
eating,
biting,
gnawing
and then sleep.
The resilience of Sleep,
till drugs make
sleep
come.
Listening to
Paint it Black
on repeat.
The people on the block
would like to believe
that if they sleep, and listen
with intent,
the sound will
Soothe.
Because after math
comes the aftermath
listening to the woke erupt

from blocks of closed schools.
Dimly lit poisoned wells
taxed and
bruised.

The people will wake.

Right Time

If you look at it right,
you can see my bubbling skin.
Numb from lidocaine.
The pain is beautiful,
like an open wound.
It reminds me of my arm.
And when
I fell.
I heard a crack.

Then nothing.
Just numb.

I almost lost it.
It was summer and I
had been wearing
a sling.

I had a tan line where
screws came in
and out.

Numb.
Infected.
A nurse came every day
to stick a swab
deep in it
to scrape out the infection.
To scrape down,
scraping bone.

That was real pain
with
a happy ending.

In what once was a
            comfortable home.

Comfortable Home

While you retreat
to your comfortable
home,

I wait
for her call.

While you retreat
to your comfortable
home,

she takes off her clothes.

They scream
and
throw roses.

She soaks in it
like a sponge.

While you retreat
to your comfortable home.

I wait
for her call.

To take her back
to her comfortable
home.

Rosa

(Come Home)

She wears a veil over her face,
after all she seems slave
Slave to a man who cuts her down every time
she stands up.

Her love was real once.
Now she's just numb.

She used to strip that's where he met her.
He came into her life, said he would take care of
her.

Now they lie together in bed.

He hates her.
She hates him.

She used to write poetry.

What happened to Rosa?
 She used to bleed her pain
into her words, into the words she read to me.
Now, she's trapped in a house of brutality–
A loose-leaf family of paper trees.

She said she would leave him. That was two weeks
ago.
Her bruises are beginning to heal.

Rosa, come home.

CENTRAL

Sick Release

Writing to release this feeling.
My lungs got me breathing
chest heaving, and finally ceasing,
like life is over, so what was the reason?
You got me twisted, my brain is thinking I'm shit
but you blink your eyes, and I fall for it.

Man, I'm blocked, writing like how I talk, working
12 hours, listening to songs in the key of flowers
wasting my time on the train.
Waiting for the insanity to subside
Let work wash out of my brain.
I know I don't really exist.
Just a ghost of my former self.
Writing this shit, and who really listens?
Poets are poets but money makes the musician.
The occupation of paying bills, working 40 hours
Staring at a screen getting fat at my desk.
Is this it for me? Losing breath, and sense of self.
Respect like the world doesn't.
Maybe I should just get drunk
listen to some shitty music
that made it platinum
While I fake like I'm something
But still at the bottom—

She Just Got on the Train

She just got on the train.
She just left my brain.
She walks towards me.
She walks away from me.
She sings songs in a different city.
Under smoky lights, and I'm alone
and don't feel right.
She strips for a living.
I stare at a book with stupid drawings.
Man, I wish I was Henry Rollins.
Maybe Leonard Cohen,
Maybe.
Maybe I wish I was smoking, reef smoke
in the ocean.
I wish I existed on your list, but
I only exist on mine.

I'm dead.

I wish the sky would light up with fireworks,
I wish I was a constellation and celestially speaking,
give me a reason to keep on breathing.

Seeing demons in my dream, speaking in my ears.
Wasting away with fears. Downing beers, drinking
tears
like the salt of the sea.

I am only alive on paper.
Once the pen ink dries out... I die

Another Episode?
Are You Giving Up?

Fuck that! Bring it to the top,
and lets bump it!
I'm sweet and off key like a trumpet—
like a piano broken and tired—
a phone disconnected and then rewired.
I'm wired for sound, listen to me now!
Now listen, I'm back.
To putting down my writing, thinking
like a musician, Fuck it!
You don't want to listen? Drink to put your piss in?
Because you're thinking is negative.
Squeamish like a sedative, a sad kid,
Sick of being sad. Get mad!
Grab the mic and show 'em what you have!
You want something?
Take it.
Don't live your life alone wasted, pasty basshead!
Not bass or bass, too many schools of fishes.

Slit wrists heal. That's my deal.
You don't like me?
That spells trouble, because your deep as a puddle,
and just as temporary, because you dry up quick
when you try to write like this.
A magician with a big wand, big fish in a small
pond.
A Timmy, a Thomas
writing rhymes being honest.
Saving Game Seven, like a game of Seven Up,

I tapped you,
put your hands in the air.

Wake   the   Fuck   up!

Wake the Fuck Up

So, you're not happy with your life?
Me too.

You know me? I know you do,
I've been too nice for too long.
You know what? I'll kill you in a song
and revive you like a psalm.
(Man, I need to find God, I've been down too long).

People don't like me, that's cool.
Call me what you think I may be, or who I am.
But I'm up on the mic, and your standing, or sitting
But I'm up here you're listening, and maybe you're
thinking,
I can do better than him, then step up kid.

You want it?
Come and get it.
My flow might not be the best
But you best respect it.
Sick of being neglected like Wexler.
Dropping quarters in a pay phone, with no answer,
Smoking pack after pack to cure my own cancer.

I am the man on the mic.
You're my private dancer.
This is Boston,
And I'm on the train, rolling down to Harvard
And back to Davis.
To get myself back and relax into the weekend.

You?

You   are   not   paying   attention.

You Are Not Paying Attention

I'm going to keep writing till, you learn the lesson
that I'm teaching.

Poetry to me, is a life source—
an ocean—
a heart beating.
And peace is pain,
and we all feel
something
sometime.

That's why poets like you write   and rhyme,
because
we sing and climb up hill.
I'll keep writing this like it's my will.
I'll give it to you.

All I got.
I got a bunch of notebooks.
And a lighter to burn 'em in my plot.
Bury me with these pages
Cause it represents the three stages,
Born breathing, live with reason.
And when you cease to be,

The last words out of a poet's mouth
should be poetry.

I'm not going gentle into that good night like Dylan

Thomas,
Flip it Bob Dylan, "Knockin' on Heavens Door,"
Annabel Lee, Edgar Allen Poe
Keats *Ode to a Grecian Urn*

Every word of Bukowski
Henry Rollins' anger and Leonard Cohen's Truth
These are the poets I strive to be.

Never been published, cause I'm missing something,
something…maybe when I die, they'll see me.
Let my words rotate the world.

Let my mind feel peace.
Put me in the urn and let me learn
that sometimes, it's good to shut up.

Let love (release), stand up and be
counted. (Peace.)
Pound the pavement (streets).
Never stop and never give up.

Now let me pass the mic to you, see what you can do…

Remember

Remember why we do this for?
To put poetry on the refrigerator door?
Like A+, look at what I did
that what it was like when I was a kid.

Now we play with toy guns, run on sentences,
Pretentious Pooches Rob us, and make us poetic losers.
We drill to the core of the earth with poetic bullets
and a steel drill.
That's the will I have. Signed and dated.
Undead, I roll on, strong like a granite wall.
Oddball, sense one, out to take it all.

The traffic on this train has made me cease to be.
Too much coffee in the blood stream, this ice
cream dream, starts to melt.

Remember, this is the will of a one-man-magic trick.
A magician on a mission
thinking diligent, and insidious, insignificant
procreatic and I am the toy in the attic
causing all the worst, destroying all
those dreams I had as a child.

I am just a wrinkle in time, on a high-speed-space-
line-driving-towards-fast food.
And some school.
I am a magician.

Remember that, Poof is this your card?
Poet pulling the rabbit out of the hat.

Finalize

Those eyes you sparkle with,
they finally split my spine.

The gift you give me
to let
every thought out and play backgammon,
like baggage in my brain,
                              check it.

This is an electrical storm
and my index is in the outlet.
Shout it loud, how proud you get
when a lyric works like a lynx
on a warpath, like an aftermath
of subsidiary flows, writing with a diligent eye,
                              finalized.

Looking down a pipe, lighting the crescent and ride
the wave,
like a static shock out of a speaker.
A stereo canon, Pachelbel meet Machiavelli.

Who do we reach?
When we pretend not to see all the grand majority
of stoners and spotters in a storm
of father's daughters, order up a whiskey and
water, blankets, snow storms,

man the storm, the one that bruises you.

Man The Storm—
The One That Bruises You

Those tears you cry, when you try not to.
Those sparkles on your eyes, their eyes glued to
you.
Those thighs in the sky as you examine the stars.
Hanging from your heels
It's not Aurora Borealis she sees when she stares
up at the sky,
It's the whisky and water getting her high, keeping
her up.
Like one more highlight is like a mudslide.
Wake up in the morning, the dawn of a new
beginning.
A stringent taste in your mouth.
Coughing smoke, walk in to the bathroom of your
apartment, see the garbage
The toxins feel so cathartic, but now lethargic little
you, can't find out what you need to do
So why not an early line? Motivated only for a
second, to clean up and get dressed.
She goes on and lets the water run over her body.,
the glitter it still stains her skin now rough with
cuts on her knees from grinding on the ground.

And her name is, Arial, is her alias, honestly, she's
been doing this so long sometimes she forgets
what her name is.
I saw her the other day; she gave me a hug and I
asked her how she's been and what she's doing
now. And she walked away back into the street.
That was last week.

Mechanics of a Poem

Mechanics of a poem.
Bring it to my shop.
Or leave it alone.
You want your style focused?
Then bring it to the shop.
Like a frustrated motorist.
Like grasshopper watch the lotus flower.
Pick the stone from your palm.
I'll show you the world above and beyond.
Whisper a secret, don't say it too loud.
I promise I'll keep it.
My ear to the ground so you can hear
the footsteps.
Listen to the engine sound.
Listen to it purr.
Now listen.
Time to rewind your style.
Change the world with each rhyme.
It just melts right to the page.
This ink is easy,
like summer breeze in a lover's evening.
It's never ending just another place to start.
Reread the words.
Pick each word apart, till the engine starts.

Almost at Davis

It's been a long time coming
running from the love,
the somber song.
A street musician strumming.
Writing from nothing to something.
Walking on a tightrope.
Nope nothings moving.

Just swimming to a distant shore.
Trying to find improvement,
wasting time, look at the clock.
Frozen at 3:00 am.
That's the words she whispers when the clock
hits ten and
the day starts again.

That's the somber song.
One word written at a time.

Late

It's about 10:30.
I was supposed to be at work at 8.
I feel like a jerk, couldn't be any worse.
Safe to say I'm late. I guess I'll work till 7 tonight.
And I will be back to write.

On the same train, this train of thought.
I'm only at Park Street. I hate going into work late.

So, I went to the doctor to talk to her.
First off, this kid comes in, a pre-med, intern
student or some shit.
I hate when I start to talk and you start typing.
Every. Word.
So basically, the med-student was like:
Go to bed early, your sleep needs "hygienic
attention."

I think it's the fact that I take enough medication
and neglect attention to my body, and the way it
functions.
I need structure, wake up at the same time, begin
to wind down around 9, and fall asleep at 10:30...

Nice poetry, sounds like a diary.

Anyway, no more alcohol and weed was Marie's
diagnosis.
The med student asked if I had problems with my
attention and I was staring at myself in the mirror

like I was rethinking resuscitation.
And again, he asked again.
"Do you have problems at work with attention?"
I said "Yes but only when I am staring at the screen,
or have an erection."
(I really didn't say that.)
Mainly I was thinking, I am getting fat at this desk,
short of breath climbing up the stairs, they want
me to take a sleep study, I don't want to sleep
overnight and then wake up to quacks drinking
coffee.

So basically, I'm late as the title says. And I need to
fix my meds. Or quit the caffeine, stop drinking
suds, and smoking bud, and everything else.

Anyway, this med-student, with a baby face looked
at me and said, "You need better sleep hygiene,
wake up the same time every morning".
I listened to his story about ten minutes. Till he
asked me what I would do, I said I will go to the
doctor and get her opinion. And I will.

I'll see the doctor soon. That kid though. That little
med student zit face, probably be driving a
Mercedes soon. Making the ladies swoon. That's
what I was thinking after he left the room. Now it's
noon.

And I will walk into my office with
my tail between my legs,
with a doctor's note,
and a fistful of meds

HARVARD

Fistful of Meds

I can barely keep my eyes open.
I'm tired as hell, and my headphones are broken.
I'll be wired for sound.
When you hear me speak this, but right now I'm
slow to the punch, but still can't be defeated.
I'm at JFK UMass, T-stop right before Quincy.
Paying for last night, the dream bug bit me, and got
me a little tipsy.
An angel asked if she could fold her wings, and fly.
I said come get me.
And in the dream, I don't remember much, but
waking up late for work, and that always sucks.
So, where was I?
The winged angel with cut wings learning to fly.
I haven't said it enough but I love this writing stuff
too much to ever give it up.
Though my profession at day is placing PONS and
fetching down CSRs, I know I'm in the right place,
when I step up to the mic and get on the stage.
Pull out my pen and radiate.
Speaking words of truth.
And Truth Be Told, I got this in my soul like Mingus.
Come on Jesus, come back in my life like seeping
blood. Back into my wrist.
Letting loose the illness in cold shadows.
I release and tackle each word like a debate team,
or a linebacker,
Say shit about me dude, it only makes me madder
Motivates me to write faster. Like my words are
glue, and they stick to you long after I'm gone,

they'll be haunting, like a spirit in the air. Light a
Spirit if you care.
Come along for the ride. Let it all out let the waves
subside and crash on the audience. I don't want
compliments, honest. I want to be known for
something other than cleaning up vomit, and blood
like how I used to be. Drinking poison,
methylphenidate, but yeah once I was a custodian.
A long time ago, now I work for a phone company,
testing phone calls...

"Hello? You there? Sorry, wrong number."

I must have made a mistake because
I chose to call you, instead of letting my think tank
explode and letting it all go. This serious flow mixed
with the blow of slow smoke from a slowpoke of an
American Spirit.
8 Hours overtime.
To make my mind exhaust itself, and ignore all
these people on the train.
Let the pen move and melt and stop at the last
sentence.
Pay attention, working 8-7.
Working out aggression.
And everything else I forgot to mention.

Beautiful/Simple

I see a beautiful girl in front of me,
It's simple to see, she seems like it's so easy and
she doesn't try hard.
Blond hair, Chuck Shoes.
Reading a book—
She hasn't gotten off at Park Street, and our eyes
haven't made contact.
She just sits reading patient/
beautiful/simple.
I wonder what her voice sounds like.
Those chucks are faded.
I don't think she wears them for fashion.

Writing

(On the Train)

I think I need new scenery, this peace I feel fills my
body with energy, till I can't see the ghost in the
shell—
The bullet in the barrel of reality.
I need to stop smoking, coughing up something in
the morning, smoking during the boring mundane
of my day.
And then smoking to fall asleep.
I wish I could keep these promises to change.
I need to change like my clothes, a new world.
A new outlook I suppose.
Yesterday I rocked the show, my hands shaking as I
read.
The ink that bled onto the pen.
Changed in me like an allergy to medicine—
An allegory of the man in the cave, once you see
the sunlight, you can ignore it or explore it.
Make a change, it can save.
Like an emperor with no clothes.
I probably won't tell you the truth, but Truth be
Told, when I find the blue waves and the green
trees,
and taste the rain outside of the forest, I'll come
back and...I'll keep it real,
and I'll keep it honest, like sunny mornings and
cancer.
Feel something, whether numb or needing to be or
feeling the breeze in an out when she breathes.
Or seeing my lungs seize while I grasp for air, but

the waters too deep and no one cares. I hope that's
not the truth for you. I may feel like this, like my
mind is an abyss, missed practice, and practiced.
Writing poems with slit wrists, then with limp
wrists, then with closed fists, but really, I think I
write the best like this. Feeling your soul flow
through me like a steady freeze, and see the
images for what they are,
       practiced moments out of focus.
After I blink and growl, show my teeth,
and that only shows madness and the ugly a reason
to see me as a reason for medication. I am a
breach in the normal synapses, a poet who don't
write raps. And listens to hipper hop and classics,
than hipsters with headphones in the back of the
class.
       I hate math! I hate meter! I see the lines and
spaces, and see the empty faces, the ugly scowls,
people give me when I walk down the street. I only
show my teeth now when I eat. I am an interesting
subject of science. A message of religion and
defiance. Kind of a combination, of what I need to
feel and what I feel is real. And all that other shit is
overlooked. As I write my thoughts down in this
book. For more than 3 stops, I feel free. And it
always leaves me in the end. Leave me alone with
                    my sadness.

Sadness

When I feel like this, I want to give up everything.
The world has made it clear, that they don't want
me here.
Too many things need improvement.
My love is leaking like a bathroom sink, all over the
apartment.
My eyes are welling up, and I feel the flood.
Why do I feel like this? Just because.
I fail when I try to change my life.
Wonder why I am alone and have a lover by my
side.
She says she wants a house and marriage, I just
want to heal my heart, too much damage, caused
by the smoke and the heartache of knowing that I
am nothing without her.
But I have nothing to give, I'm empty.
And at work it's just as worse, I wear a noose-neck-
tie
And don't deal with anyone but disconnected
phone lines.
And when I get a voice on the phone, I don't say hi.
I hang up. And then I make another call, over and
over again. Listening to my mind going crazy and
my heart beating.
And then it's lunch time and I have a few laughs, a
sandwich, a smoke, and then go back to
disconnecting phones.
I guess I'm just sad. And now it gets bad to worse.
I'm 31 and feel ready for the hearse.
Been cursed since birth to deal with this mind of
rhymes and recorded sirens. I'm sick of who I am,
and who I could become, but I am numb and wish I

could tell the truth to someone, that this mind is a
time bomb and
            my love is a gun.
Time to go back to
disconnecting phones, and then go home and feel
really disconnected.

Dying to Be

This rehearsal life, this photograph is fading.
Not much light to shine, the contrast is off.
The world is a flower and each petal has been
picked
and dried out on a gravestone.

I am one of a bunch of flowers trampled on by an
overzealous God, or a villain in the heart
running each game,
    you can't beat the house.
Walk out with nothing but a sad smile.

My gravestone will be:
              Tried hard, but not enough
                  for you to remember
                     me.
This world of threes, this disease this distaste,
debased.

The time stamp on this life overdue on this book.
A vessel that sank too soon.
A world of mad hatters, and only one Alice.

This world is no wonderland.

Ev-olution

(Listening to *Evidence*, "the Layover")

Now let's begin. Let out everything.
Bring back the vibes and let me ride.

Think back to a better time.
When the mind was practical, fantastical,
Magic like fractals, spastic like empty stomachs,
Flow like blood vessels, fly like pterodactyls
And bring it back Mac Dad Delicious
Ready to finish this without a witness.
Grab on tight and listen to the brilliance, of a man
in a gray suit poised to make millions.
Sick of dead last finishing. Here these other cats
and what their spitting.
Some sounds good and I can't recreate it.
But when space is low, time gets wasted.
And the demons in your head, you got to face
them.
And if Emcee's try and damage me, can't phase me.
Because what you lack in symmetry, I make up with
energy.
To the last drop is gone.
I am going to rock poetry and hip hop
Get on my soapbox like a republican, and say shit
that sounds like truth to them.

I talked to a cat, and she said meow.
But for real dude, the dog barked and said you got
to get loud.
Listen real intently to each dramatic scene.

And stay in the lines on your notebook.

Already beneath underground, cause I look like a freak.

Last call. Got to take a shit, but you're occupying the last stall.

Wanted to play b-ball but some cat said I couldn't hack it.

That was back then.

What you say now to a game of one on one?

Real truth hits when you're spitting lyrics.

But when no one can hear it, do the words disappear?

Evaporate into air?

Like all the air in the crowd, when I stand up on stage and read page after page of words I put on paper?

It's the undertaker.

The unemployed waiter.

The broken cab driver with a pair of pliers, and a box cutter to slash your tires, Boss.

I'll get fired, and I can move on, I'm playing chess, Place your own PONS, cause I looked around the meeting, barely breathing, listening to some sucker sucking semen dreaming about a 4-day weekend. There's more than that, I got an arsenal, the world is like a carnival, and I am a marvel super hero, Mortal Kombat, Fuck it, I'm Subzero.

Let the Spirit Move You

See I've lost a lot in my time.
Lost my mind a couple of times.
Lost cousins, and family members
to Cancer, lost a world I never knew,
but now I am going to get on top of her, and
love each minute, till I'm finished.
This world seems like shit, but listening to the
realest music, got your seeds in it.
I got a hip hop stop watch to tell me when it's been
a minute.
It's been a minute, time to kick in the door and
move in.
See you all have money, and I want some, cause
living for crumbs is stupid and dumb and I'm no
bumbling crook, not stealing pagers, listening to
the news, reading the papers, my eyes are like
lasers shooting through like x-ray vision, listening,
got my phasers on, you willing, I'm dealing. A new
hand, not to sling rocks but sell mix tapes of poetry
and hip hop on your block. Sell magazines on CD,
3$ dollars please to hear my poetry, listening to
man the storm perform at the open mic.
Like me on Facebook, but not in real life.
Cause you'd never really like me in real life.
I'm weird, I'm odd, listen to hip hop and folk rock.
I stay in the spaces, don't drift on the lines, don't
drink the water, only whiskey and lime.
This is my time to shine.
This is the time to get on the mic and let loose my
mind.

hip hop on the ones and two's. I like your shoes,
let's fuck and let loose, let the spirit move you and
time to go,
Train stop.
nice to know you.

So that's what I am doing, showing improvement.
Reading lyrics like a student, listening to Emcees
and following the pace and the movement.
The CSR life is not for me, just give me a mic and I'll
put it loud to the crowd, with music and melody,

Sense of Self

(laundromat poem)

Division bell singing like a rhythm king listening.
Like a soldier standing
Like the lover's dancing
Like a mirror glass
I reflect myself in the image of
tattered clothes, overgrown, tattooed and
overdone.
Sense has lost his self again, feel totally exposed.
But more alone like hiding my horns in my baseball
hat.
Like I really don't know where I stand.
In this lake and land.
I drown on both grounds.
Batter up, fast-ball-curved hat-you're out.
It's amazing how fast you lose all respect you've
gained.
Thought you mastered your brain, but now more
insane.
But this feeling of mediocrity grows on me like
weeds.
And if you cut me, what would come out?
I would like to believe ink, but really, I'm just a pig,
or a dog, and I am locked out

This is how I feel…at a laundromat.
I need to find my sense of self.

Friday

(Need Peace/Want Sleep)

Working is done for the day, got a lorazepam-free head
and crazy, well see, where I'll be.

Crazy on the microphone, amplified headache.
Making me lose control, a seismic shift, an earthquake.

But still, I kill at will, each word of a sentence represents still.
Mental ability keen life like Keaton, scene's I'm stealing.
Shady as Em, but have no reason to be.
Wish I could flow like EV
But that will never happen.
I'm a rocket rollercoaster. Got my feet tapping to the rap and rhythm
Listen, quiet, silence, reading resilience, breathing defiant.
Crazy, what happened to Dog, Dirty Lion.
Give him a call and we start the engine.
Pump the gas, stretch the limbs and legs, rolling on a rhythm, that doesn't make sense.
Every life I know, I wish I was one instead of 3.
Cause when my mind gets low, I flow and fly out of this city.
But I stay in the same place.
Glued to the root, sadness on my face and bitter is this drug that life gave me.

But I'll keep it cool, till one day I leave.
See, my dad, told me that life is infinite.
That it doesn't stop, but when I die, I'll call his bluff.
Enough pain in my head that this mental that flows
temperamental like one day a soldier, next day a
general, swallow a grenade, step on a landmine.
I don't like my life but it sticks to me like glue.
And what you say sticks to me, until I come
unglued.
Sometimes I let it go, feel nothing like endo smoke.
Like nothing y'all ever know, sad as I am, sick as I
might be, the illness of medicine, keeps me sick
and pasty, like my skin.
Medicine makes me lower than grass. And you are
the mower.
I make me feel like a piece of shit, sick of all the
diagnosis, of people who don't know me, let them
condemn me.
I never meant to be anything. You made me.
This is your pain. I just need and want, need peace,
want sleep.
Need a lorazepam and a place to go.
These are my dreams.
Nothing gold can stay.

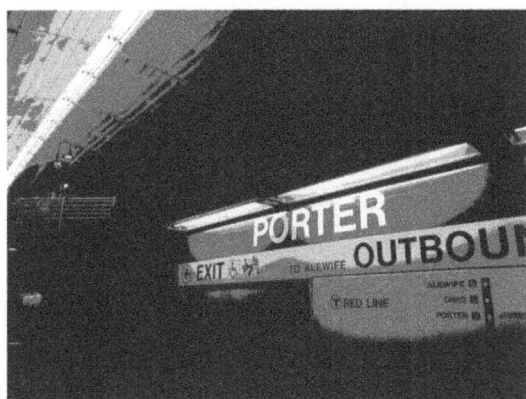

PORTER

Well Wishes for
Sleeping Fishes

Wake to the alarm clock,
Ringing seven o'clock
I got my phone, don't use my watch.
Don't need no locks my mind is freed–open.
And each thought rings out like a bell siren.
Without warning, in the middle of morning, like an
old man snoring away his boring day.
Getting hired and fired in the same day.
That's the way my day went today.
      Well wishes for sleeping fishes.

Don't you know that they never close their eyes?
Like a new dad? Or security guard like my friend
Paul?
Or like Clockwork Orange? Keep the villain's eye's
open.
And damn like Bam, the man comes back like a
sandwich.
 A quiet dog is a docile bitch.
Like if a stitch in society I'm unweaving, then
what's the reason I am screaming
out my mind man?
I got to get a clue, take a lorazepam.
Got to get a clue cause I am bored of your games.
Your monopoly means shit to me.
I'm going to build up Baltic and Pacific Railroad,
and you can rent on my house…but anyway.
Ability and flows, cause once you get to Park,
there's no limit to the fines when you step on my

property line.
So, well wishes for sleeping fishes.

Don't you know that fish sleep with one eye open
like clockwork orange or a polaroid frozen, right
before I blink you take the damn picture, then I
look like a Picasso when Van Gogh, I go with it. See
I like poetry call me Walt Whitman.

I dig people who can hear the noise that's on the
railroad.
I like a sound of applause in my area.
Instead of something being lit, then being
destroyed.
Jump on the grenade man and there I go.

Wake up the sleeping fishes. Tell em, I'm coming
home.
And all that's left is a solitary boat, with a little man
    drowning,
        trying to stay afloat.

Roses are Red, Violets are Blue

So a lot of people don't get poetry,
this poem is for them...

Roses are red, Violets are blue,

this is the beginning of a poem
you've known since childhood
this is the beginning of a poem
when people used to say
that poetry began with this lame phrase.
So confused are people about who poets are
and what they do
and only know Poe and Dr. Seuss.
Some people need a new introduction
to the written word,
welcome to the warmth of the earth,
you've known poetry
since the day of your birth
and continue to know it.
Listen to the words on the radio
flowing from a hi-fi stereo
each word was scribbled down first,
on pad from paper from papyrus
and you listen to it,

that's another notion about poetry;
That its only for boring intellectuals who use difficult
verse to describe a mundane universe
of words.

Then there is the difference between snapping and clapping.
There's really no difference,
both showing love.
One sounds a little too pretentious,
and the other is the human response
to words that move you and make you feel something,
different then you're used to.
Then there is the classics
everyone was forced to learn in school,
to be or not to be, do not go gentle into that good night,
the pledge of allegiance,
all words all poems,
all have different meanings,
but I don't want to lose the audience,
back to the beginning.
Roses are red, Violets are blue,
but before I go
Let me tell you:
Poetry is for everyone who has words or worse to
worry with,
everyone has this talent to do this,
so when someone says poetry is for pretentious idiots,
it is, but it is also for
the spiritualist
the activist
the hip hop kids
the linguist
the wordsmith
the worse for wear
and the neverdids
the headbangers

the wallflowers
the muscle head
and brain dead
potheads
the patriot
and the anarchist
the tame and the loud
the free
the shackled
the ashamed
and proud
the lover
the martyr
the show stoppers
and the ticket takers.

Poetry is for you listening
and me writing this
little list
of people I'd like to see join
Me.

The community needs you.

Fuck Roses are red, Violets are blue,
if you think that poetry is that
then you might want to read this one again,

or pick up the pen,
I guarantee you'll feel something,
and if you don't,
well, that's your opinion.

However stupid.

You're entitled to it
and I'm entitled to write a thousand poems
to disprove it.

All you need to do is write down a sentence or two,
and then two more,
then let your mind go
and damn,
you'll be looking at a poem

and you can thank me when I see you again.

Or Email me.
Email is good too.

Bells

Got to go back to where I was.
Where each word mattered, and it was all about
love.
Where a song bird sang, and this is what she sang
Get back to the beginning and let the bells rang!

Let the bell ring while they still got timing
Where the world looks like a gold mine shining.
Brilliance defined, and back to the beginning.
I got rhymes…. here my DJ spin.

Now back to the skills I bring, I'm no dumb shit.
Might be ignorant to the fact, that I ignore all the
problems that I have.
But whether or not, God can forgive
That's what I am betting on because I'm not strong,
Walking around all types of seasons, tired, close my
eyes,
Rest the demons.
And my lungs are breathing, cause I quit smoking.
But I'm not lost, I'm not broken.
Chilling on the train, on a locomotive.
Waiting for rhythm, and a little bit motion
Looking for emotion to perfume the air.
Running through the nose, like flows out the
nostrils.
Rhyming off track, just got on track again.

Cause we got the hook, captain, and the beat if you
want it.

What you waiting for drop it, like 18 banners in Boston.
Like waiters on the Charles, like last call at dive bars,
Strippers at the club bouncing down and up for some of that green stuff.
Drop it like a yellow card in soccer, like a flag in football,
Like my accent, like this stream of thought
Listen to Preemptive Strike, and that's what I do before you get a chance to. Break off a beat and a rhythm. See what moves you, moves me too.

Some Ole Bull Shit

1.
Slow down till we stop.
That the truth, the gift you got.
Is to speak to the beat,
And until it drops,
I'll write poetry but my heart beats hip hop.

2.
This quackery, insane tragedy, realizing life is a ball
game and writing don't get a jacket, this is the
championship, and if it sounds tragic, you're
sweating now, and the ball cap don't fit.

3.
I'm going to write till I start to make sense again.
When 1 was one and 10 was ten, and you could
either write fast in time with the pen, or you could
write smart and drop gems.

—At one time I was fine.
—At one time I could write.
—At one time I could read the signs.
—At one time the world was mine.

I can't write with a beat. I can't write if I can't see.
I can't write and only measure defeat.
In the arms of the one who haven't quite caught it.
I can't write without alcohol, but I'm not an
alcoholic.
Can't write without vegetables but me I am allergic.

Can't write without curved wings, but to you I'm just an addict.

Can't write to save my soul, the devil's dogs are playing with it, tearing me limb from limb, I can't fucking do this.

I can't see anything; I have a blind man's vision. My thinking is far from liquid, got to spray it all over the page, push forward, press play.

And jump on stage, say fade away to the welcoming wind, and rule the day with a chicken wing, or a gold ring, or everything and nothing, This bullshit I am writing. I'll make sense on the next page. Goddamn this shit.

The day's frustration.

SENSE

I need a plan.
Something that says, here I am,
I'm the man.
I guess I missed the program,
And been down so long.
Depression's just another name
for what my eyes see, when I stare
at the mirror in front of me.
And even if I could walk away without being beaten
my mind will have these seizures, and soon I will be
seeing nothing but stars, and
a solar system.

Watery Eyes

Watery eyes,
Programmed lies in my head,
like programming a television set,
first, I pressed record and made things happen,
then can't rewind, so here I am a wrinkle in time.
Lost like a traveler, rewinding each rhyme like a
clock
making each word talk from the back of the
suburbs, to the dogs on the block, who see nothing
but a cell block, or could rot like me, and rewind
the clock, again to the time where I could rhyme,
and stand behind it.
But I am lying to you.
My skill is dying.

Rancid

Is it this pen or has my flow gone rancid?
Read a book about how I should write, now I'm
stuck, lost energy like
Symmetry on this planet.

Like this world,
Like this job,
Fuck a job, kills your creativity.

Free Prose
#200,000,000,000

Late night walk in the park.
Reading rhymes, writing lines down to make my
mark, and if my shirts need starch, then my boss is
a shark but leave it alone, and relax to it.
Jazz music.

Where the world kind of starts going at a million,
and you're thinking about all about your feelings,
and you feel stupid and useless, relax to it...jazz
music.

If you think back to the beginning of jazz.
It was about disconnected harmonies.
In perfect time, where everyone would hit it in a
perfect style and flow together, and their flow fell
sick...
Relax to it...jazz music.

And on the train the most hectic place, where
there are so many people and so many faces.
So many examples of love and hate, and your all in,
Chillin' to the twist...relax to it...
Jazz music.

And when you wonder where it all came from
Like hip hop and who your favorite Emcees
influence is,
9 out of 10,
it will be jazz music.

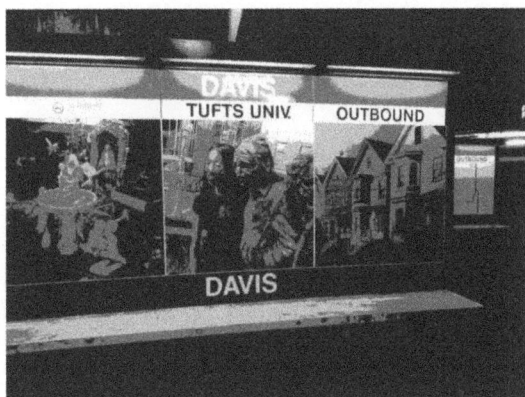

DAVIS (home)

Blue Note

Damn, Listen to Coltrane
and when you come back,
let me know how the blue train was, cause you
might come back a blue note, a blue poet,
or a shiny star dated and translucent, and then you
will know what it is and why we listen to it,
oh, love that jazz music.

Salem Poetry Trials

Witches are stupid;
Poets kind of are like witches.
We all stick to our covens
our cauldrons
our magic wand.
But I couldn't get down with witches.
Back in Salem
when I was falling asleep in a crawlspace
PBR left out to warm
ready to drink in the morning
where I talked to the TV and
branded myself blood brothers with Andrew
where I left one morning
nights and nights without sleeping
and decided to walk myself right into
a hospital
Salem rock city
that day after where we would walk to the park
with our guitars
and showcased new songs
at yellow dogged cafes
where I would meet my friends and share songs.
Oh how I loved them.
I was sick then
and didn't realize it.
I'm sick now
but I deal with it.
A lovely illness
where unchecked you become
solitarily confined to your own madness.

I thought I would feel something up here
with all these wonderful poets
but I am not one of them
I write for life
even in the mix of their cauldron
I still didn't fit the mix.
I always feel that my words are my life
and if I don't share them with you
we will remain strangers
and within all these poetic parlor tricks
I am writing alone
on a park bench not a
friend to share this with.
I am alone
in my own ugliness.
On a beautiful day
I still feel sadness
it's a lovely world
I'd rather be in this lonely
wolf pack
then a shadow beneath your feet.
I'd rather be alone with my thoughts
Then the stars.

The Song Remains
the Seized

Who will read this?
I am not sure if my tempered words
hit hard
or are ever heard,
I am not sure if what I do makes a difference
or if its coincidence that I exist
in an instance,
and settle for long distance marathons,
a hunters paragon,
Lex Luthor's lexagon,
I want to—only for a minute.
So I lubricate my ears with music,
I settle down and breathe in
the beautiful air,
no longer a toxic bloodstream
I flow on mixed feelings
and bottle up emotions
with double meanings,
I want to shout my presence to the earth,
I want to embrace the mold of my former self
and take away its hurt,
I want to dream that I don't have to take medicine
to tame my liquid thinking,
I want to dream that I am winning
and this world will go into extra innings,
I want to be.
And I never can be.
I want to see, but I am blinded by threes

talking forests of winter trees
coughing up fluid,
exposed to the world,
a matrix birth,
a sight to be seen from the doctors hands,
the cold breath of a winter world.
Wishing I could see inside myself
and see the truth.
The end of the pendulum
and the story of the seized.

Misfits

Microphone mathematics
see the smile disappear
as I rewind and listen
to my fear controlling the pen
I move.
To another world.
back to the instincts, I make
misfits mix with liquid
till they sick with it.
Can't control this rhyme scheme,
I'm lost in the machine.

Smoke Free Soliloquy

Back to the beginning, writing at the end of the
inning. People watch me, they watch the way I
move.
What am I trying to prove? Nothing to you.
Lose the attitude, you don't like the way I rock, well
I see you, what you think of this? People see what
I'm seeing frozen, still breathing. Still cool in my
mind erosion. My mind needs erasing, a seizure, a
cold compress.

I'm just releasing pain from my brain, Who were
those cats? What's wrong with me?
Thinking that they don't like me, cause they know
mac and cheese and sense one the AC and all the
negativity surrounds me like a battle of bridges.
Writing rhymes don't see the quickness. Because I
quit smoking and burned all my bridges and
nicotine patches? Quit smoking, they say, you'll
feel better, but what is this world that revolves
around me in dry weather? Stand and sit down,
lost and found. Fuck, need an Ativan and a mind
transplant, an avalanche of dirty dances, and world
whiplashes, people hate the rhetoric that goes on
with this cigarette deprived derelict, this simple
stiff upper lip, where people think this shit is hip,
my existence, is fleeting like a warship. I would love
to believe that I could see my savior write in front
of me wish my manic ramblings had a reason to be.
I hear footsteps, they're right in front of me,
getting quicker to the middle finger, saying fuck

with me, and you will see. But whatever today is a good day to die. Crazy on the Microphone, Bi-Polar, Schizoaffective, holding on to shit, I wish I could grasp, but I don't understand, why I'm even here man. Conduit for destruction and disaster.

I wish I was in Norway. I see a picture of Iceland Air, and I wish I was there.

Just Another Page
In My Rhyme Book

Take another look at this pasty kid, with eyelids
dim, looking like the wind been knocked out of
him.

Like he can't live, like he's going to be sick from
some bad tuna fish.

That's right I do feel ill from lunch still, only cost 4-
dollar bills.

Dunkin Don't, damn I feel like I'm bloated still, and
it wasn't no donut.

I had my coffee, I'm going to change the subject
cause it makes me nauseous till I think about it,
and I vomit all over this train,

By the way, this heat on this train is like Miami in
winter,
Never been, but dream about it now again.

I can only imagine, like Jon Lennon. Legend like Jon,
Little like Wayne.

Writing like fireworks going off like a shotgun,
releasing each word like a garage hero, or a guitar
band, it doesn't matter where I flow, through rain
or snow from shallow water to a full flow food.
I'm going to write rhymes cause ink is in my blood,
and I'll never give up.

Might Not Write Enough

Might not write enough
But I love it still.
Love like a new born baby,
And a prisoner's last meal.

Thank You

To my friends and family for sticking with me.

To Lisa for being right by my side.

To Dad and Mom, for giving me this mind.

To TJ Edson, Chad Parenteau, Andrew Borne, it's been a wild ride.

To Jill Hunter Burrill and Mrs. Todd, who believed that I could write, and gave me the tools in school.

To Andy O'Brien, Ryan Heroux, Randy Jackson, Adam Meaney, Nick Vlachos, and Matt Carey.

To Ben Selchan, Mike Vaughn, and Dan Amicone for giving me the nickname that would fuel all my successes.

To the great people who have met me halfway, to Mark Kariotis, Amy Lenar, Sabine Mautner, Jen Mirabella, and Steve Vicidomino.

To Karyn Morrison, Sarah Heroux, Liza Zayas, Thomas Gagnon, Elaine Denenberg, Chad Parenteau and TJ Edson for creating the oddball foundation.

To Grace Crain, Julia Monz, Brandon Hicks, Rob Beatty, Kris Dipietra, Catherine Bonner, Tim Gager, Joshua Corwin, Elaine Hall, Rachel Applebach, Doug Holder, CC Arshagra, Zwamby Bennett, Will Hall, Oryx Cohen, and Jennifer Knight for all your help along the way.

To the memory of Amanda Wilding, the architect behind *oddball*, may you rest in peace.

To the memory of Pete Geraghty, you are missed, and

you are loved.

To Michael Cherry, may you always be 27.

To Andrea Cherry for being the strongest woman on the planet.

To Jon Wright, my brother who I love dearly.

To Amy Gatto my sister. You make this world a better place.

To Cameron, Amelia, Jimmy, Julien, Averi and Alexander—you are the future.

Finally, to the people who live well in recovery and choose every day to rise above all limitations: Don't let anything stop you. You are strong, you got this. Keep going.

About the Author

Jason Wright is the editor and founder of *oddball* magazine (www.oddballmagazine.com). He is the author of *Train of Thought: Poems from the Red Line* and *Letter to the World*. He is the president of the oddball foundation. He has a dog Obi, and a very patient, loving wife. He is a lucky and grateful man.

Other *oddball* Publications

*9 7 8 1 7 3 3 9 9 9 8 4 7 *